GEORGE BEST

THE LEGEND – IN PICTURES

Dedication

To Suzanne, James and Daniel who enabled me to appreciate what is really important in life.

First published in 2006 by
Appletree Press Ltd
The Old Potato Station
14 Howard Street South
Belfast BT7 1AP

Tel: +44 (0) 28 90 243074
Fax: +44 (0) 28 90 246756

Web site: www.appletree.ie
Email: reception@appletree.ie

A catalogue record for this book is
available from the British Library.

George Best: The Legend - in Pictures

ISBN-13 978 0 86281 853 1
ISBN-10 0 86281 853 2

Desk & Marketing Editor: Jean Brown
Editorial Work: Jim Black
Designer: Stuart Wilkinson
Production Manager: Paul McAvoy

9 8 7 6 5 4 3 2 1

AP 3350

GEORGE BEST

THE LEGEND – IN PICTURES

IVAN MARTIN

Appletree Press

CONTENTS

"Great stuff George. Give it to me,"

Denis Law screamed as his Manchester United team mate George Best ghosted past two defenders.

The expected pass never came. Another opponent was left floundering. Law's cry went out again.

"George! George!"

Still his pleas were unheeded as George rounded another defender and cut inside.

"You're a greedy wee.......
Ah, great goal George!"

"Thanks Denis,"

said Best as he was engulfed by Law and several other colleagues.

"I knew you were offside!"

Such were the joys of playing with the most complete footballer ever to grace British football.

THE GEORGE BEST STORY

George Best had everything: supreme skill; boundless energy; the ability to make and score goals; radar-like awareness of the game as a whole. But in an era when pitches were often like ploughed fields he had grace and balance which seemed to allow him to skim across the mud and float through the mire.

He was also one of the bravest players ever to step onto a football pitch. At a time when referees gave players little protection the game was full of hard men whose sole purpose was to prevent the most skilful players from performing. Best took the knocks and rarely complained. Whether it was Norman Hunter at Leeds, Tommy Smith at Liverpool, Dave Mackay at Spurs or the particularly ruthless Ron 'Chopper' Harris at Chelsea, Best never flinched.

His courage never faltered. One of the best examples of this came in an evening FA Cup tie at Old Trafford against Chelsea. George picked up the ball at the half way line near the dug out. He set off on a diagonal run leaving the Londoners defence in his wake. As he got to the edge of the 18 yard box Harris hit him like an express train from behind.

Best stumbled momentarily in the mud and then danced round Peter Bonetti before planting the ball in the net. It was a goal that demonstrated his tenacity, bravery, ability and clinical finishing. The celebrations, as he dropped to his knees in front of the Stretford End and looked heavenwards, showed another of his compelling assets. His sense of theatre.

George Best created the Theatre of Dreams at Old Trafford. He was the shy, homesick schoolboy who became a superstar. The soccer sorcerer of the swinging sixties.

The Belfast Boy was the first soccer star to cross the bridge into showbiz. He had the looks. The fast cars. The dolly birds. The lifestyle. But above all he had the talent.

So special was that talent that George Best was rated the greatest footballer ever. Arguments could be put forward for others. Pele. Maradona. Cruyff. Di Stefano. Puskas.

All of these players had a special magic. A God-given ability that set them apart. Just to be part of this elite group guarantees worldwide adulation. Choosing the best seems impossible.

But Best was best. The person who handed him that accolade was Pele. The Brazilian, who sprang onto the international stage at the World Cup in Sweden in 1958, gave George the ultimate accolade.

When someone as revered, respected and remarkably talented as Pele talks about soccer the world sits up and takes notice.

Speaking at a dinner in New York, where he remains a cult hero from his time with the Cosmos in the NASL, the great man saluted the Belfast Boy.

"George Best was the greatest footballer of all time," declared Pele.

From a room containing not only some of the world's finest players but several members from the Brazil team rated the best ever for winning the World Cup in Mexico in 1970, that statement echoed around the globe.

George was the greatest! Had that been said by even the most respected football commentator or journalist in the world it would not have had the same gravitas.

But Pele was rather more than a respected figure – he was somebody who had been there and done it at the highest level. One living legend acknowledging another.

When George was asked if he really was the best player in the world his response was instant. He broke into that famous smile, looked straight at the camera and said.

"Yes I was the best player in the world."

Then he laughed and with that characteristic twinkle in his eye added, "Well Pele said I was and who am I to argue with him?"

Vintage Best. Milking the moment. Enjoying the compliment. Quite happy to accept the accolade. But

George Best was far too sharp to ever be drawn into a spurious argument about who was the greatest.

He knew in his heart that for a time he undoubtedly was the finest footballer on the planet. But he also knew that just being mentioned in the same breath as Pele, Maradona, Cruyff, Di Stefano and Puskas proved one thing beyond all reasonable doubt.

He was one of the all time greats. The genuine article.

George Best was born in Belfast on 22 May 1946. His parents Dickie and Anne lived in the east of the city at Burren Way in Cregagh. He played football for the local boys club and although small in stature was big in talent. At 11 years old he won a scholarship to the local grammar school Grosvenor High. It was a rugby stronghold where soccer was taboo. Separated from the game he loved George was unhappy in his new surroundings. He began to play truant.

George was soon caught out and after discussions between his parents and the school it was agreed that it would be in everyone's best interests if he moved to Lisnasharagh Secondary. He immediately settled there. He was happy to be reunited with his old mates from primary school. But most of all he was delighted to be playing football again

Right: When this picture was taken in October 1965 George Best was nudging towards two years in the Manchester United first team. He was a still a mere 19 years old. In that short time his rise had been as meteoric in football terms as the emergence of The Beatles had been in music. The 'El Beatle' madness would occur within six months but at this stage George could still enjoy being a mere celebrity rather then a star. Once he had taken Benfica apart in the Stadium of Light in Lisbon the following March George's life changed. That is when the hysteria kicked in. Lines of girls screaming at matches, others inconsolable afterwards because George had been spirited away through a back door because the police felt unable to guarantee safety. The fan letters poured in – 15,000 a week most of the time. Neither football, nor Manchester United, had ever seen anything like it. Suddenly soccer had become showbiz!

with a round rather than an oval ball.

Like most kids from east Belfast with a talent for football George came to the notice of Glentoran. In a move akin to Decca turning down The Beatles they did not pursue their interest in George, feeling he was too small.

However Bob Bishop who had been the Manchester United scout in Belfast for many years saw beyond George's puny physique. On seeing young Best in action he immediately sent a telegram to Matt Busby the manager at Old Trafford. A modest man not given to hyperbole his telegram was one Busby would never forget. It read

"I think I've found you a genius."

George joined Manchester United as an amateur in 1961. Within two years he had made his first team debut against West Bromwich Albion at the tender age of 17.

His opponent that day was Graham Williams, a craggy Welsh international full back with a reputation of being something of a hard man. George ran him ragged.

Afterwards Williams approached the youngster. He shook his hand and then delivered the now immortal line,

Left: The most enduring soccer friendship of George's life was with the Scottish international he called simply 'The Lawman'. Denis Law had joined Manchester United in 1963 following a spell in Italian football with Torino. George watched in awe at Wembley that year as he scored one of the goals that helped United defeat Leicester City 3-1 in the FA Cup final. It was the club's first trophy since Munich. Shortly after the cup final George signed his first professional contract with Manchester United on his 17th birthday, May 22 1963. Within three months he had made his first team debut. By the end of the year he was in the side to stay. The pair are pictured coming out for a game with Tottenham in September 1966 at White Hart Lane. Denis' doleful expression is probably explained by the fact that he was still in a state of official mourning after England had won the World Cup some two months previously.

"Stand still son so as I can have a look at your face. I've been looking at your backside all day disappearing up the touchline."

George Best had arrived.

But being the wise old owl that he was Busby knew not to rush him. He immediately was dropped into the reserves again but he had laid down his marker.

Even at this stage the homesickness which plagued George's early years at United was still a problem. At the very start he and another local youngster Eric McMordie had done a bunk back to their homes in Belfast. George's parents were glad to see him and were even prepared to contemplate getting him a trade in his native city. But Busby had other ideas. He knew that Bob Bishop's initial assessment had been correct.

So George was tempted back to Manchester. But the club arranged frequent visits home as he struggled to make the transition from Northern Ireland to the industrial heartland of northern England.

The young Best had not only caught Busby's eye he had also come to the notice of the Irish Football Association. He made his debut in the green jersey of Northern Ireland when he turned out for the Under 18 youth team in 1963. He was just 16 years old. Nine days shy of his 17th birthday when he lined up against England at the inauspicious surroundings of Oldham's Boundary Park.

Norman Kernaghan, known in his playing days as Shirley Temple because of his flowing, curly hair, was in charge of the team from Ulster. Until Norman Whiteside came along he had been the youngest ever player to win a full international cap for Northern Ireland.

As he watched the scrawny kid from Cregagh with the trendy Beatle haircut weave his magic the pipe smoking Kernaghan was heard to remark, "he's like something I'd clean my mouthpiece with".

But with full time training Best was getting stronger. He was at his happiest with the ball at his feet and was always last to leave the training pitch. From early on he established a reputation as one of the best trainers at the club.

During Christmas 1963 George had been granted permission by the club to return to Burren Way to spend the holiday period at home in Belfast. United's Boxing Day game with Burnley was far from his thoughts as he relaxed in the bosom of his family. Then a telegram arrived from Busby.

It requested that George return to Manchester immediately to play in the first team. Burnley had inflicted a 6-1 St. Stephen's Day defeat on Busby's boys, hence the SOS to Cregagh ahead of the return fixture at Old Trafford.

Showing remarkable bottle for a 17-year-old with just one league game for Manchester United on his CV, George assured the club he would be delighted to pop over and play against Burnley – provided he was flown back to Belfast immediately afterwards! That was agreed. Burnley was duly defeated 5-1. George scored his first goal for the club. He would never again be on the fringes of the first team.

At 17 George Best was a bone fide Manchester United player. The newest Busby Babe.

He then became the catalyst in the United team that would win two First Division championships and the prize most coveted by Busby, the European Cup, by 1968.

But before that, and after just fifteen first teams games for United, George made his full international bow against Wales at the Vetch Field. It was the Spring of 1964. His room-mate on that trip also made his debut against the Dragons. He was Pat Jennings, who went on to win a record 119 caps for Northern Ireland.

The pair, described later by Martin O'Neill as "the only world-class players Northern Ireland had when I made my debut," could not have been more different. Jennings was a colossus of a keeper. His speciality was plucking crosses out of the air with one of his shovel-like hands. But he was a great shot stopper too.

Best, waif-like, and weighing in at around 8 stone was physically in stark contrast to big Jennings, who before turning professional with Watford had made his living felling trees.

What they had in common was the ability to make the game look easy. With Big Pat in goal opposition forwards knew they had a problem. With George they usually had an even bigger one!

Right: In the autumn of 1967 George and Mike Summerbee of Manchester City and England fame went into the rag trade. The two footballing friends opened a trendy boutique in Manchester called 'Edwardia'. This very public friendship turned business partnership did not go down well with some of the diehard supporters at United and City. But the boys reckoned their shop was bound to be a winner as the United fans would come because of George while Mike would attract the City supporters. When George left Manchester Summerbee continued in the fashion business. He set up a company that specialised in hand made, tailored shirts. It exists to this day. The 1967/68 season saw Manchester as the football capital of Europe. United did not manage to retain their First Division title, in the end they lost out by two points to City. But the blue half of Manchester's bragging rights were short-lived. Within a month United had become European champions and the first English club to lift the European Cup.

"He was the complete footballer, gifted and hard working," enthuses Big Pat. "He was the finest player I ever played with or against. I treasure my memories of him even though on occasions he made me look rather foolish."

"Everyone knows about the Gordon Banks goal that was disallowed at Windsor Park. Well he did the same against me and the goal stood!"

That 'goal that never was' against Banks was typical of George at his impish best. The England custodian had returned from the 1970 World Cup in Mexico as the undisputed number one keeper in the world.

His save there from Pele's header had heightened the legend and was subsequently to be voted the greatest of all time. Fast forward to the following May in the Home International championship: Northern Ireland versus England in Belfast.

When Banks threw the ball out of his hands to kick it upfield Best was there in a flash to toe-poke it over his head.

With the England goalkeeper in hot pursuit, he headed it over the line. The referee controversially disallowed the 'goal' for dangerous play. But footage of the incident clearly shows there was no infringement. So much for the luck of the Irish!

Left: When George was playing interest in Northern Ireland games always heightened. His autograph was considered the Best one to get ! Add that to the fact that England provided the opposition and things were building up to a frenzy when this picture was taken in April 1970. George was seldom out of the headlines. Two months prior to this he had scored a double hat trick in an 8-2 win over Northampton in the FA Cup. Those six goals remain the most ever scored by a Manchester United player in a single match.

Although he played a mere 37 times for his country, scoring 9 goals during that thirteen-year spell, it should have been 10. George always added to an international occasion – especially at Windsor Park. When he donned the green jersey there the minnows of Northern Ireland were given instant hope. The expectancy in the crowd was so intense it could be felt around the ground. When George got the ball the noise level used to rise by several hundred decibels. Never more than the day he virtually defeated Scotland on his own in 1967 at Windsor Park.

The Scots came to Belfast with a star-studded line-up that included Denis Law, Frank McLintock, Tommy Gemmell, Eddie McCreadie, John Greig and Bobby Murdoch. But Best simply took them apart. With Gemmell having a nightmare chasing shadows around Windsor Park the Scots switched Chelsea hardman McCreadie to man mark Best.

His attempts to stifle him met with no more success than those of his unfortunate colleague. Suffice to say that Northern Ireland would have won by a much greater margin had it not been for the efforts of keeper Ronnie Simpson.

He was the second best player on the pitch that day bringing off a string of superb saves. He was finally beaten by a low drive from Dave Clements after Best had bamboozled the Scottish defence for the umpteenth time.

Award winning sports journalist Malcolm Brodie, who has seen every Northern Ireland international since the war, was amongst those mesmerised by the incomparable talent of Best that day.

"Without doubt it was the finest individual performance by any player ever to grace Windsor Park the spiritual home of Northern Ireland football," enthused Malcolm.

"Scotland simply had no answer to George's balance, his ability to dribble the ball at speed and his determination to take the game to them."

"His performance that day is part of the folklore of Northern Ireland football. It is remembered simply as the George Best international."

At that stage George was just 21. He had already been part of the Manchester United side that had won the First Division title in 1965. That got the club back into Europe.

Not only was this First Division championship success the club's first in nine years – it was extra sweet because it was the first since the Munich disaster of 1958 that had decimated the Busby Babes.

George was the fresh face of Manchester United at this stage. Significantly younger than Bobby Charlton and Denis Law he provided the special additive to the mix Busby had created. He was now a genuine top-flight player.

But all that changed one night in 1966. United were back in the European Cup. It remained Busby's holy grail, his determination to win it heightened by the sense of loss after Munich. The club's quest took them to Portugal to play Benfica. Eusebio and his team had lost the first leg at Old Trafford and things looked bleak for United as the headed for the Stadium of Light. Portugal had not been a happy hunting ground for the Reds. Two years previously they had been trounced 5-0 by Sporting Lisbon in the very same stadium. Benfica had never lost a European game there.

Enter George Best. He had the game virtually over with two goals in the opening 12 minutes. He then laid on another for John Connelly. Busby's boys won 5-1. Best grabbed the headlines and 'El Beatle' was born.

"It was the night he changed from just being a football star into a huge celebrity," recalled Pat Crerand. "The match was a high point for all of us. But it ensured that life for George would never be the same again."

What an astute observation that turned out to be. When George returned from Portugal, sombrero atop his head, it was like the return of the king. He had moved from the back to the front pages with 90 minutes of magic.

"For people who knew what a fantastic player he was it was inevitable that something like this would happen one day," reasoned Crerand.

"He was such a fantastic talent that it was only a matter of time before he faced up to a big match like this one and took the opposition apart."

That match signalled to the world that George Best could do that. He did it again in the international against Scotland in Belfast mentioned previously.

George Best superstar was to be the blue touch paper that illuminated United at home and abroad. In 1967 the

Right: This is George in full flight for Northern Ireland against England at Windsor Park in May 1971. The match in the British Championship was played against a backdrop of heightened civil unrest. Northern Ireland lost that game 1-0 but managed wins by the same score against both Scotland and Wales. However one month previously George had illuminated Windsor Park in a European Championship qualifier. Cyprus provided the opposition and the Belfast Boy produced the magic. He scored his only hat trick for his country in that game. The other goals coming from Jimmy Nicholson and Derek Dougan.

championship again ended up at Old Trafford which meant another crack at the European Cup the following year. United battled all the way to the final at Wembley and ironically their opponents were Benfica.

That night George Best superstar made Busby's dream come true. On a muggy May evening in extra time with the score at 1-1 the Belfast boy took control. He raced through, rounded the Portuguese keeper and nonchalantly rolled the ball into the empty net. It was George Best in his pomp. The greatest footballer on earth.

Manchester United went on to win the match 4-1. But the key moment was George's goal. He had allowed Busby to finally live his dream. Only those in Old Trafford's inner sanctum knew what that meant to the man known simply as 'The Boss'.

Sadly for George and United that was the pinnacle in football terms. Best was surrounded by a largely ageing team. Bill Foulkes, Shay Brennan and even Bobby Charlton were getting a bit long in the tooth. Denis Law was increasingly troubled by knee problems. Indeed he had missed United's finest hour because of injury. The time had come to rebuild a new United around Best.

Sadly that call was not heeded.

Left: When this picture was taken in September 1971 George Best was Manchester United. The Reds defeated West Ham 4-2 that day and George dominated the game scoring a hat trick. He was effectively carrying United along on his back. It was now a team of ageing stars and young players who were not quite up to the mark. This was because they had been thrust in too soon or were simply never going to be able to cut the mustard. George had been devastated when United had failed to land Mike England and Alan Ball following the inevitable break-up of the European Cup winning team. These were the calibre of players he knew were required to make United great again. Even George Best could not do it all on his own. Well not all the time !

"It should have been the beginning of a wonderful career," George later recalled. "Instead it was the beginning of the end."

After Busby retired Wilf McGuinness, Frank O'Farrell and then Tommy Docherty tried to recapture the glory days for Manchester United. All failed miserably. George had a patchy relationship with all of them. None had the father figure influence on the wayward son that Sir Matt enjoyed.

McGuinness probably fared best. O'Farrell never really fitted in at the club while Docherty's ego ensured that he and Best were never going to be a marriage made in heaven. George always felt that Docherty went back on his word during his last days at Old Trafford. The pair fell out big time and George walked away from the only club he really loved for ever.

Despite the hurt and pain this caused him he knew that the team the Doc built was but the palest of imitations of the one that Busby led to European Cup glory.

"The philosophy at United under the Doc was quite simple. You draw some, you lose some," George once caustically remarked.

The bottom line was that mediocrity and George Best were mutually exclusive. At 22 he had been European and English footballer of the year. Within five years he had gone from Manchester United and the club would wait almost two decades before Alex Ferguson brought the glory days back to Old Trafford.

After leaving George retired more often than Frank Sinatra. But he kept coming back. His most productive spells were in the United States, at Fulham and for a brief spell in Scotland at Hibs. But compared to the champagne days at Manchester United it was all flat beer. The irony of that would not be lost on George who had ongoing problems with alcohol throughout his life.

The problems caused a lot of angst to some of those nearest and dearest to him but the one who suffered most was George himself. Eventually his health packed up and he died on 25 November 2005 at a mere 59 years old.

Like so many sportsmen George was never able to replace the smell of the liniment, the roar of the crowd and the adrenalin charge that can only come in the heat of the game.

Some will portray him as flawed genius. That is their prerogative. But at the end of the day those who saw him play will remember only one thing – the joy of his pure and extravagant talent.

"When the football was great and I was playing well, I couldn't wait to get up in the morning and that was the foundation of my life," he once remarked.

Perhaps his late mother Anne hit the nail on the head when she said simply, "With George it was always the ball". Now that he has passed on to the great game in the sky all that remains are the memories of him with that ball.

As ever, he was perceptive enough to realise that. "When I'm gone people will forget all the rubbish and all that will be remembered will be the football. That'll do for me."

When I was asked to write this book something Brian Kennedy said to me immediately came to mind. Brian, of course, sang at George's funeral at Stormont. He managed to do so under extremely difficult circumstances with immense dignity. He told me later that it was, "a privilege to have been asked". I must say I felt exactly the same about working on this book.

I am sure as you work your way through it, the wonderful photographs of George will trigger numerous memories of the good times. The glory years.

George Best was an icon before most of us really understood the meaning of the word. His ability as a footballer has been unsurpassed. His impact still lingers on.

Not too surprisingly it was that most erudite of journalists, Hugh McIlvanney, who summed up that extra special quality George had, that no one else in sport, never mind football, has ever matched.

"George Best made people feel good," said Hugh.

I couldn't have put it better myself!

Ivan Martin
Belfast, December 2005

"When I'm gone people will forget all the rubbish and all that will be remembered will be the football. That'll do for me."

— *George Best*

Above: This black and white, head and shoulders shot of George was taken in December 1964. He was 18 years old and already causing a stir in the Manchester United first team. A month previously he had scored his first goal for Northern Ireland for whom he had made his debut the previous April against Wales in Swansea. It came in a 2-1 away defeat in Switzerland. George was also coming up to the first anniversary of his first senior goal for United. That had come during the Christmas fixture against Burnley at Old Trafford in only his second senior game. He had flown over from a holiday break in Belfast to play in the match. At this stage the club were still sending him back to Cregagh regularly to combat homesickness. While the picture demonstrates that George was fashion conscious even at this stage, the haircut is a lot more conventional and less Beatlesque than it was to become.

Left: George warms up ahead of a Manchester United game in December 1964. At this stage he was just about to complete his first year as a regular in the side. The previous Christmas he had been at home in Belfast when a telegram arrived at Burren Way. It requested an immediate return to Manchester following a disastrous 6-1 mauling by Burnley on Boxing Day. In those days it was common practice for back to back games to be played at holiday times between clubs situated reasonably close to each other. United won the return 5-1 and George scored his first senior goal.

Left: This shot of George in action was taken at Craven Cottage in 1964. It was the home of Fulham FC whose chairman Tommy Trinder was a well-known comedian. The star player at the club was Johnny Haynes. He was also captain of England and had stayed at Craven Cottage, despite interest from bigger clubs, when Trinder made him the first £100 per week footballer in England when the maximum wage was abolished. Haynes was also the first footballer to endorse a product when he became the official face of Brylcreem, a mousse-like product which many males wore on their hair in those days to help get it to sit like Elvis Presley's did. Before long George had joined him on the commercial merry-go-round. Hands up who remembers which were the Best family sausages? Why Cookstown of course!

Above: In mid-February Manchester United were drawn against Barnsley in the FA Cup at Oakwell. They won the game 4-1 and George scored the final goal in that victory. Note the size of the crowd and the difference in the design of the stadium compared to what we are used to these days. Although this was around forty years ago Oakwell seems light years away from the Old Trafford of today or one of the new custom-built facilities like Bolton's Reebok Stadium. As holders United were pleased with their victory in this game. Sadly they were unable to repeat the previous season's success. That year the FA Cup was won again by United – but it was the boys in claret and blue from West Ham, skippered by Bobby Moore, who took the trophy.

Right: This classic black and white shot of George was taken in November 1965. Almost six months before his 20th birthday it shows how wafer-thin he was. At that stage he weighed in at less than 9 stone. It is also notable that the Beatle hair cut had not quite kicked in as yet – but it was getting there! So was Manchester United. That season the club would pick up its first championship since the Munich air disaster in 1958 tore apart Matt Busby's legendary Busby Babes.

Above: This shot was taken on the day that United clinched the First Division title in 1965. The feeling of relief and euphoria around Old Trafford was immense. It was the first championship since Munich. That meant that United were back in the European Cup again the following season. For Matt Busby the long wait was over. He relished the challenge despite the fact that with each European trip memories of that fateful day in February 1958 were rekindled. The Reds clinched the championship with a 3-1 home win over Arsenal. George had settled everyone's nerves by banging in the opening goal when Denis Law put him through after just six minutes. Law then added two more in the second half. It was game set and match. Manchester United were First Division champions again and the celebrations could begin. George is pictured afterwards with the obligatory girl on his arm – nothing unusual there! He is wearing a trendy, well-cut jacket – nothing unusual there either. However his decision to top it all off with an old fashioned Belfast duncher was obviously him taking the Michael. I mean it was far too early for the grouse shooting season!

Left: George sporting a fine example of what has become known these days as the 'classic' Manchester United strip. The red jersey with the round neck in white with matching cuffs, the white shorts and red socks. You will note also the absence of even the club badge from the shirt. As for any sponsors name that was still light years away! The only thing which would have appeared on George's shirt would have been the number 7 in white on the back. Perfectly colour coded!

The Legend – in Pictures   29

Left: George played 37 times for his country. He made his Northern Ireland debut against Wales in the Spring of 1964. Six months later he was off to Lausanne for a World Cup qualifier against Switzerland. It was in that game that George scored his first Northern Ireland goal at the Stadium Olympique. A Swiss photographer captured the moment for posterity as George leaves the home keeper Elsener helpless and watches as the ball hits the net. Sadly the Swiss snapper managed to get neither the ball nor the net into his picture. But at least he managed to include the scorer!

Above: This was the definitive image of George Best returning to Manchester from Portugal after he had destroyed Benfica in a European Cup game in 1966. The 5-1 scoreline reverberated around Europe. The Portuguese champions had never lost a European match at the Stadium of Light before. George simply tore them apart. The second goal of his hat trick was described by the respected journalist David Meek, formerly of the Manchester Evening News, as the finest George ever scored. After the game Matt Busby confessed he had instructed his team to keep it tight in the opening half. In the words of Bobby Charlton, "George had the game over after twelve minutes." Perhaps he had not been listening to his manager's team talk! He returned to Manchester a hero. His days as just another player were over. George Best superstar had been born.

Left: Not yet 20 years old George is pictured ahead of a First Division game at Stamford Bridge. It is March 1966 and this was his first match back in England following the demolition of Benfica. George had been dubbed 'El Beatle' by the press in Portugal. It was a tag that Fleet Street was quick to mirror. How appropriate that Best's first match back should be against trendy Chelsea. The allure of the Kings Road lingered with George all his days. In later life, when he was doing television punditry and working the after dinner circuit, he based himself there. As can be seen in the photograph the Belfast Boy was still a bit on the scrawny side. But he had proven that he could do it at the highest level. The Beatle haircut, which was to become his trademark, was not quite perfected though!

Above: In the mid-60s George's flair on the pitch was matched by his feel for fashion. To use one of the in phrases of the day he really had the knack! In this photograph George makes final preparations with some models ahead of a fashion show at Tiffany's nightclub in Manchester. The event was to showcase the latest George Best collection. It was the autumn of 1966 and George was just 20 years old.

Right: A pencil-thin George Best is pictured at White Hart Lane before a league match with Tottenham Hotspur in 1966. Matches against Spurs gave him the opportunity to link up with his Northern Ireland room mate Pat Jennings and also England international Jimmy Greaves whom George rated big time. "Jimmy was undoubtedly the greatest goalscorer amongst my contemporaries," Bestie once remarked. "And arguably the greatest ever in the domestic game." The pair shared a waspish sense of humour. Introducing George at a function following his liver transplant Greavsie told the crowd, "It's great to have George back. He's a changed man. I mean he's turned up for a start!"

Left: This happy scene shows the Manchester United team who had
clinched the First Division title the previous week with a 6-1 win at West
Ham. They were presented with the trophy ahead of the final home
match of the season against Stoke City. The basis of that title success
was an unbeaten run of twenty games from mid-December which
allowed them to hit the front by mid-March. That season John Connelly,
who had been part of the '65 title winning team on the right wing left for
Blackburn Rovers. Two youngsters Jimmy Ryan and John Aston came
into the side. Aston played on the left so George, who could play
anywhere would move to the right. Ryan, preferred the right, so when
he was in the team George reverted to the left. Aston eventually won
the battle for a regular place in the starting line-up and was part of the
European Cup winning side the next year. Ryan remains at Old Trafford
to this day as part of the coaching staff. He played in that match against
Stoke.

Above: This picture of George having a shot saved by Chelsea keeper Peter 'The Cat' Bonetti in November 1966 is interesting. It shows what a run-down place Stamford Bridge was even in those days. Ken Bates rebuilt the stadium and created Chelsea Village but that exercise nearly sent the club to the wall. Enter Mr. Abramovich and suddenly Chelsea had no money problems. Back in 1966 they had the makings of a decent team with Bonetti, Eddie McCreadie and John Hollins the players in George's vicinity. Bestie reveals that Bonetti did not get his nickname because of his agility. "He was called The Cat," insisted George, "because every time he saw Jimmy Greaves in the penalty area he had kittens."

Above: A picture of its time if ever there was one. The United players celebrating in the bath after winning the First Division title in 1967. I just wonder what the current United players or their rivals Chelsea would think of these scenes from 1967? It is hardly what today's footballing millionaires have come to expect. In the bath from left to right are Denis Law, Nobby Stiles, Shay Brennan, Jimmy Ryan. Bill Foulkes, Bobby Charlton and George. They were obviously expecting someone would snap them in the bath because Nobby has his teeth in! Who can forget him dancing around Wembley after winning the World Cup looking like an extra from a Dracula film. Professional at the top level was a different world back then. Paddy Crerand, one of the senior players at the club and a seasoned Scottish international was on a basic wage of £65 per week. I remember George once saying that he was not exactly sure how much he earned a week at United. He explained that he was earning four or five times more from outside activities. It was these commercial activities which broke the ice for today's players. George was the player who not only moved football from the back to the front page he also made it part of the entertainment industry. These days when top players can earn more in a month then some of the past players got in their careers it would be easy for old professionals to feel resentful. George never did. But then he never cared about money to begin with as anyone who actually knew him would surely tell you. For George life was an adventure which he embraced and lived to the full. Those who criticise him, especially for effectively quitting top class football before his 28th birthday, have little to do. In his time at United he played 466 games and scored 178 goals. He was top scorer in 1968 and scored more than 20 goals a season five times. How many of today's players will end up doing that? His critics tend to forget that George was a first team regular by the time he was 17. He played at the top for ten seasons. The other thing is that over thirty years after he left United he remained one of the most instantly recognised people associated with football in the world.

Above: Once he established himself in the first team at United George was able to indulge his liking for sports cars. Some of his choices show that style was much more important to him than 'oomph'! Take the car in this picture. It was a complete eye-turner. It was a Lotus which could go a bit but was totally impractical and very much of its time. But George tended to change his cars regularly. He had other Lotus models, a Jag saloon similar to the one made famous by Inspector Morse, and several of the classic E-type Jaguars. MGs also featured in his late teens. But a sportscar that really caught his fancy was the Sunbeam Alpine. Not particularly powerful, it had classic lines and really looked the part – the ideal car for a famous young footballer to take his girlfriend of the time out in on a Friday evening. Her name was Carolyn and she was Miss England at the time. Despite her fame she still lived at home with her parents and George rolled up to the house in his Sunbeam Alpine. He was invited in and after exchanging pleasantries with her parents left. He was still sitting in his car outside fifteen minutes later when he heard a tapping on his window. It was her Dad. "What are you doing son, why are you still sitting there?" he enquired. Sheepishly George explained that he had a puncture and had no idea where the jack and wheelbrace were kept in his new sports car!

Right: This rather arty picture was taken in one of George's Manchester boutiques a month after United had won the First Division championship in 1967. In the championship run-in George had scored a hat trick against Newcastle United. That brought his total for the season to 10, not bad for a winger. But the following season, as he increasingly assumed the mantle of being United's key player, he rattled home an amazing 32 goals. He went on to be the club's top scorer for the next five seasons. Everything in the garden was rosy for the 21 year old superstar. He was the star attraction for the best team in the country. He was a fashion icon who by now was setting rather than following trends. But better still he was about to go off on holiday to his beloved Majorca!

Left: This picture from February 1968 will evoke memories for people of a certain age of 'Spot The Ball' in the *Ireland's Saturday Night* every weekend. For the uninitiated, the ball was removed from the picture. Then you had to guess where it was and mark that spot with an 'X'. If you managed to successful place your 'X' in the centre of the ball you won a cash prize. The game is Tottenham Hotspur versus Manchester United at White Hart Lane. George, surprise, surprise, is centre stage having a shot on goal. The two teams must have been sick of the sight of each other by this stage. They had been drawn together in the FA Cup a few weeks previously. United had home advantage but the game at Old Trafford finished 2-2 with a youngster called Martin Chivers getting both Spurs goals. Spurs won the replay but not the FA Cup which went to West Bromwich Albion courtesy of Jeff Astle's goal in a 1-0 win over Everton. United were not too bothered though as they made Wembley anyhow to win the European Cup!

Above: Looking every inch 'El Beatle' George is pictured at Highbury ahead of a First Division clash with Arsenal in February 1968. At this stage of the season United were still in with a chance of retaining their First Division title but there were other priorities. They were still in the hunt for the European Cup which Celtic had won the previous season in Lisbon becoming the first British club so to do. Having lost the opportunity to be that United wanted to ensure they would become the first English club to win it. That duly came to pass the following May.

Above: In the Spring of 1968 Real Madrid came to Old Trafford for the first leg of a European Cup semi-final. The Spanish giants had slipped from the glory days of Puskas, Di Stefano and Gento which had brought them the European Cup in the first five years of its existence. But they were not the side of style and grace that they had been. Their main objective in Manchester seemed to be – 'Stop Best at any cost'. As the photograph shows, George was on the end of some rough tackles. Inevitably he responded in what he believed was the most effective way. He scored the winner in a 1-0 victory! The burning question after the game was would it be enough to take to Madrid for the return. In that game United were 3-1 behind at the interval. David Sadler nicked a goal back from George's cross which made the aggregate score 3-3. Then the unlikeliest of players, centre half Bill Foulkes, trundled in an equaliser to leave United 4-3 winners over the two legs. Even without the injured Denis Law the Reds had managed to make the final. Busby was on the brink of his dream.

Above: Being voted Player of the Year by the football writers has always been an honour players cherish. But George's award in the 1967/68 season was particularly sweet. Firstly he became the youngest recipient ever of the coveted award. Secondly the award was made before United went to Wembley to lift the European Cup. This picture shows George with Matt Busby at the Café Royal in London just after it was presented. Two weeks later Busby would get the prize he coveted above all others at Wembley. That European Cup success clinched the European Player of the Year award for 1968 for George. So it has to go down as the year he won the treble!

Left: The date this picture was taken is etched forever in the minds of the Manchester United faithful – 29 May 1968. It was the day that Matt Busby's dream was realised when United won the European Cup. This is the pivotal moment. The time when George Best showed why he was the footballer who moved another Northern Ireland legend, the great Danny Blanchflower, to remark "the kid has ice in his veins". It is the moment when he slipped the ball into the Benfica net in extra time at Wembley to set Manchester United firmly on course for victory. The purists will argue that we can see neither the ball nor the net. They miss the point. What we see is George watching the moment the ball crosses the line. We also see the look of hopelessness on the faces of the Benfica players left in George's wake. In the background we can also see a wafer thin youngster who that day celebrated his 19th birthday. He was Brian Kidd. Manchester born and bred. A European champion before he was out of his teens and he scored as well! I wonder which he regards as his best birthday ever?

Above: This photograph was taken on 30 May 1968. The morning after the night before – the night when Best had helped Busby live his dream. Manchester United left Euston station to return north to a massive welcome in their own backyard. But for once they were also embraced by Londoners as the first English club to lift the coveted European Cup. Flanking the soon to be Sir Matt and helping him to hold the trophy are Pat Crerand and Georgie Boy. Winning the game had taken a lot out of everyone. But they perked up when Joe Loss and his Orchestra played them into the banquet in the Russell Hotel with Phil Coulter's 'Congratulations'. The party was still in full swing by the time the United group reached Euston to take their private train back to Manchester. On their return they took the trophy round to Denis Law who was in hospital for a knee op and missed out on the big night.

Above: This picture was taken at the end of United's 4-1 win in extra time in the European Cup final on 29 May 1968. George and Bobby Charlton embrace, ecstatic at the triumph. The interesting thing is that their delight was essentially for Matt Busby. Charlton had survived Munich so it was especially poignant for him. George enjoyed a special relationship with Busby. The United godfather knew that in George Best he had a talent that would have illuminated any of the three great teams he built at Old Trafford. Such was the legend that had built up around the Busby Babes that it seemed no player coming after them would ever be in the same league. Until George.

Above: This is the official Manchester United team photograph ahead of the 1968/69 season. It was the one after the European Cup win and George is hidden away in the middle row between Paddy Crerand and Francis Burns, one of the new kids on the block. The season could be summed up with the old cliché that after the Lord Mayor's show comes the dustcart. United never touched the heights of the previous season. They finished a miserable 11th in the First Division, losing as many games as they won, fifteen of each and drawing the other twelve. It was their lowest league placing since George had come into the side. Scant consolation was a decent run in the European Cup which saw them loose out 2-1 to AC Milan in the semi-final. But the empire was crumbling. The Busby era was over and life at United would never be quite the same for George Best again.

Left: George, Pepsi cola at the ready and booted and suited for the return trip to Manchester, after United won the European Cup. He was signing pictures of himself for young fans ahead of the train journey back up north. United frequently used trains in those days. Something today's players would scarcely be able to comprehend. Can you imagine Rio Ferdinand, Wayne Rooney and their pals travelling back to Old Trafford by train? Better still, can you imagine them winning the Champions League? Me neither.

Above: The rivalry between the red and blue sides of Manchester was never more pronounced than in the late '60s. Both United and City had good sides with the Reds' blessed trinity of Best, Law and Charlton being countered by the Blues' triumvirate of Lee, Bell and Summerbee. Inevitably George did things in his usual unconventional way. One of his biggest pals in Manchester was Mike Summerbee the City and England winger. The two even went into the rag trade together. They are pictured here in Santa suits with a bevy of football followers. The one immediately behind George is Eva Haraldstad, a former girlfriend of George's who would have liked to be a lot more.

Right: George is pictured here ahead of a 6th round FA Cup tie against Everton in March 1969. Since winning the trophy in 1963 the club had not come to within a bagel's jowl of another success. Hopes were high ahead of this game but they were dashed when the Toffees recorded a 1-0 victory. To add insult to injury, Everton then lost to Manchester City who went on to win the final against Leicester with a Neil Young goal. For United the wait for FA Cup glory extended to 1977.

Above: This classic picture from March 1969 sums up the life and times of George Best in those heady days. It was an FA Cup 6th round tie at Old Trafford and after a disappointing season was the Reds last grasp at glory. The FA Cup ended up in Manchester that year. Sadly for United it was won by City courtesy of Neil Young's goal in the final against Leicester City. But this shot shows George on the ball, that wonderful balance there for all to see, against a backdrop of Old Trafford stuffed to the gills with row upon row of spectators. Also in the photograph is Alan Ball. He once came to George's rescue when his car broke down in the Mersey tunnel after a game at Goodison Park. Travelling through the tunnel with his wife Lesley, Bally noticed George had stopped and eventually did the knight in shining armour thing and towed George to a nearby garage. The newspapers got hold of the story and it appeared the following day under the banner headline 'Best Dragged Out Of Tunnel By The Balls'.

Above: When George Best started playing for Manchester United's first team some of the players used public transport. Amazing as that may seem in today's climate of club cars, it is a fact. Agents were not even a feature. Indeed the first player to have one was George Best. He was a man called Ken Stanley who operated from a back street office in Huddersfield. Stanley was not involved with the football. He looked after endorsements, boot deals and so on. But his principal job was to try to deal with the 10-15,000 letters a week that were arriving for George. He hired a secretary and a driver for the Belfast Boy. The trio are pictured here with George, whose white Jag is behind them. It could be a still from 'The Krays'. Not that Stanley was in any way crooked. He was just completely out of his depth.

Above: The European Footballer of the Year is an honoured bestowed on the outstanding player in any given calendar year. In this picture, taken in April 1969, George is being presented with the trophy for the year that had ended the previous December. There to make the presentation was respected journalist Max Urbini. But the shot is interesting from another perspective. Beside Urbini is Bobby Charlton, wearing a suit so obviously unfit for the game against Burnley which followed. He won the award in 1966. Sir Matt Busby stands beaming next to George and is flanked by Denis Law who had been European Footballer of the Year in 1964. Considering that the journalists on the judging panel had the whole of Europe to choose from it is remarkable that three players from one club should win it three times in five years. But then when Charlton, Law and Best were in the starting line-up the word remarkable tended to appear rather regularly!

Right: This action shot of George was taken during a Manchester derby game in March 1969. It is classic Best. Shoulder dipped, ball close to feet bearing down on goal. If I wanted to commission an oil painting of George in his pomp this is undoubtedly the picture I would give the artist to work from. As it happens 1969 was something of a curate's egg for George. In April he was presented with the European Footballer of the Year trophy and in July represented the Rest of the UK against Wales in Cardiff. The downside was a suspension in December for knocking the ball out of referee Jack Taylor's hands after a League Cup semi-final against City at Maine Road. He had earlier rather harshly booked George. The Belfast Boy claimed his post match actions were "playful rather than malicious". But taciturn master butcher Taylor did not see it that way. He reported George to the FA and a month's suspension followed.

Left: In 1969 football in England was booming. The country were the reigning world champions, although it is still best not to mention this around Scotsman Denis Law! In addition to this, United were European champions and the crowds were flocking into the grounds. The biggest crowd invariably came to Old Trafford where they squeezed in, sardine like, to the terraces, as our picture shows. It was taken at a home league match United played against Nottingham Forest. George, undoubtedly the top box office draw in the country by this stage, is being given an unusual amount of space by the Forest defence. Perhaps that is why they finished fifth from bottom that year. Mind United did not fare much better ending up an inglorious eleventh. The opportunity to salvage something from the season evaporated when they limped out of the European Cup at the semi-final stage against Milan. Admittedly they were on the wrong end of some diabolical refereeing in the home leg against the Italians courtesy of a French official. But the record books show it was AC Milan who went on to Ajax in that year's final.

Above: In August 1969 Manchester United headed for Denmark for some pre-season games. It was there that George met Eva Haraldstad. He was very taken by her but as he later explained that it was all very innocent "chiefly because she had a boyfriend in tow". He lamented his fact to some journalists on the flight home and the tabloids immediately set out to find her. Soon she was in Manchester, loving her new-found notoriety and dubbed 'the striking Viking' by the Press. Eva upped the ante when she announced that she and George were to be wed. Given United's keenness for George to settle down he did not demur immediately admitting later that the idea appealed to him "for a day or so". When Eva realised George was slipping away she headed for the courts. It was settled out of court for £500 and a ticket back to Copenhagen. The episode allowed George to create another little piece of history. He was apparently the last person in England to be sued for breach of promise to marry! This photograph, taken in August '69, shows the pair sipping wine before the whole thing went pear-shaped.

Left: George Best and Harold Wilson both came to power around the same time. Following the demise of the 'You've never had it so good' years under Harold MacMillan, the Conservatives floundered under Sir Alec Douglas-Home in 1964. Wilson and Labour got elected. At that stage George had just established himself in the first team at Manchester United. If he was to become the first showbiz footballer then Wilson was to become the first Presidential-style PM. He recognised the value of photo opportunities. So he engineered to have his picture taken with popular icons of the day who appealed to young voters. He played up his Liverpool connections when he was snapped with The Beatles. In his shot it is George's turn. He receives the *Daily Express* Sportsman of the Year award at a luncheon at the Savoy in London. Whether or not the Prime Minister would have supported an event run by a strictly Tory newspaper had the award been won by an ageing footballer who was losing his hair is doubtful. Wilson was the master of spin long before spin doctors had ever been invented. George was just the master.

Above: When this picture was taken in January 1970 George had become as much of a fashion icon as a superstar footballer. He had his own line in clothing and a couple of boutiques on the go. He also had a penchant for sports cars. He tended to change these almost as regularly as his famous range of so called granddad shirts which were characterised by having no collar. His car on this occasion was also fashionable. It was an MGB GT with the trendy wire wheels – in United red of course!

Right: Just as happens today the big guns enter the FA Cup fray in the third round. Those games always take place on the first weekend of January. In this picture George and Willie Morgan are seen running out at Portman Road for a game against Ipswich Town. Some people suggested that the pair of them were quite alike. Apart from similar hair styles it is not easy to make a case for this. Harder again would be any suggestion that in footballing terms Best and Morgan were comparable. In truth Best was to Morgan as Barbados is to Ballywalter.

Above: Such was George's celebrity that he moved in circles other footballers could only dream about. He is pictured here arriving at Number 10 Downing Street for a reception the Prime Minister was giving for West German chancellor Willy Brandt. His network of friends often amazed his team mates. When he was at Hibs the boys in the dressing room were gobsmacked one Monday morning when someone asked what he had done at the weekend. "I was at a party with Tom Jones and Sean Connery," he said as if it was the most natural thing in the world, which to George it was. "Oh were ye?" exclaimed a Hibs team mate. "Well I was up at my Da's darts club. The pints is 10p cheaper up there." Ah! The perks of professional football.

Left: No footballer before or since has been embraced by pop culture like George Best. The female fans who went to concerts to scream at The Beatles, The Rolling Stones or The Walker Brothers were now to be found at football grounds. When George got the ball the screaming started. They never watched the game. Just George. He even discussed cutting a record with Ray Davies of The Kinks but Matt Busby was having none of it. George dated Lulu for a while, he was friendly with Tom Jones and featured in teen magazines like *Fab 208* as often as the artists in what was then called the Hit Parade. Don Fardon had a hit single about George called 'The Belfast Boy'. In our picture another pop hopeful Lucy Farrington serenaded him in his Edwardia boutique with her song 'Georgie'.

Left: Throughout his life George had a penchant for beards. In this sh[ot]
taken during a local derby with City in March 1970, he is seen sportin[g]
one. The City player he has left in his wake as he scampers down th[e]
touchline is Mike Doyle. He was a Manchester lad who was a comple[te]
dyed-in-the-wool Blue. Doyle hated the fact that a time when City we[re]
winning trophies, United always seemed to be able to go one better.
Before derby games he was always mouthing off about what City we[re]
going to do to United. It made great copy for the newspapers,
especially when he was less than complimentary about George Best.
The only time the Belfast Boy ever thought about it was when he wa[s]
out on the pitch. He took great delight in displaying his wide range of
skills in games against the guys from Maine Road. If, on occasions, t[his]
involved taking the mickey out of Mike Doyle then so much the better[.]

Above: No club feared George Best more than Leeds United. As we can see in this picture taken during the FA Cup semi-final of 1970 it took three of their players to mark the Belfast Boy. They are Norman Hunter, closest to George, Billy Bremner, immediately to his left and Terry Cooper in the background. All three were seasoned internationals yet none of them was rated by George as his most difficult opponent. That honour went to Paul Reaney, Leeds right back and one of Elland Road's unsung heroes.

Right: When Scotland came to play Northern Ireland at Windsor Park in April 1970 George once more dominated the headlines. Unlike the Scots previous visit in 1967 which has gone into football folklore as 'The George Best international', this time the headlines were not the sort the Belfast Boy would have wanted. On a damp, dull day he was kicked from one end of the Windsor Park mud heap to another. Referee 'Tiny' Wharton, a red-faced giant of a man, had offered him little protection. Eventually George stepped out of line and was booked. His anger boiled over and he slung some mud in the direction of the official. He also spat at the ground. Mr. Wharton decided it was a bridge too far and sent George off. George accepted later that he had over-reacted. After all being kicked left, right and centre was nothing new to him. His biggest regret was that it had happened in front of his father Dickie, his family and friends in Belfast. Our picture shows him leaving the playing area for the long walk up the Windsor Park tunnel. Despite the inclement weather and the incident that had just happened, the enthusiasm of the fans to catch a glimpse of their hero does not appear to have dampened in the slightest.

Above: This is a rare colour shot of George with his parents Dickie and Anne Best. It was taken in May 1970 when his folks celebrated their silver wedding anniversary. George had nipped home for the weekend ahead of taking his usual close-season break in Majorca. Trips to Burren Way were becoming increasingly difficult. He loved to be with his family but once the word got out that he was at home the house would be deluged with fans. George's celebrity was difficult for his parents to deal with. Dickie, as has been shown many times since, has an inner strength and quiet dignity that enables him to cope. However Anne struggled with it all. She came to dread going out because people would identify her as George's mother. It eventually got on top of her so much her health deteriorated and she died at just 54.

Above: This is the official squad photograph of Manchester United ahead of the 1970/71 season. The first thing that is striking about it is that there are no trophies in it. The previous season had been a barren one, the worst in a decade. The other thing that is missing is Matt Busby. He had moved upstairs with Wilf McGuinness taking over. But he only lasted until the end of the year and Busby was hauled back into service. But everyone knew that was only a temporary arrangement. Sir Matt knew it was time to go and the hunt was on for a permanent replacement. Jock Stein at Celtic was widely touted but in the end Frank O'Farrell came in from Leicester City. Just a few months into the job he was hit with a bombshell ahead of the Newcastle game in October. A phone call, purporting to come from the IRA, told the Geordie police that George Best would be shot if he played. O'Farrell told George it was his shout. But assured him the club would support him whatever he decided. Feeling that he had no option but to play George went ahead. He felt that if he had not done the problem would just keep recurring. As ever he tried to defuse a serious situation with a one-liner. "Typical of me to insist on playing when the manager had offered me a day off," he said.

Left: This picture was taken towards the end of 1970 in a game against Leeds United at Elland Road. There was always added rivalry between the clubs because Bobby Charlton's brother Jack played for the Yorkshire club. Also on board there was Johnny Giles, who had been shown the door by Matt Busby after the 1963 FA Cup win. His sister was married to Nobby Stiles. Add to that Don Revie's paranoia about George Best and it became a pretty potent mix. A recipe for disaster some would have said. Especially as Leeds feared the Belfast Boy on the park. George, with his flair for fashion and his showbiz lifestyle, was like an alien to straight-laced Revie. He believed in dossiers on the opposition for players bedtime reading and organized bingo sessions to foster team spirit. Not surprisingly George had a view on 'The Don'. He once remarked that, with the exception of Leeds players, all his peers who played for Alf Ramsey "had total admiration for him". Interestingly when it came to Revie, who succeeded Ramsey as England manager, there was "an almost equal lack of respect". Leeds' respect for Best can be seen by the way they always had two or even three players close him down as soon as he got the ball. In this shot it is Mick Bates and Paul Madeley.

Above: The careers of George Best and Pat Jennings are more intertwined than many people might think. For a country the size of Northern Ireland to produce two such wonderful players in the same era is remarkable. They made their international debuts together in Wales in 1964. They were always room mates when playing for Northern Ireland. But above all there was a genuine friendship and admiration between the two of them. Except when United played Spurs! In this picture, taken in 1970, George slips the ball past Big Pat to force a 2-2 draw at White Hart Lane.

Above: This picture taken in March 1971 shows George doing his impression of a seal! His ability to do tricks with the ball was second to none. In one friendly game he was breaking through the opposing defence so often that he made a bet with a team mate that he could hit the opposition bar six times during the match. By half time he had already managed five! On another occasion he went on David Frost's television show to display his virtuoso skills. After saying "Hello, good evening and welcome" to everyone Frost showed a mini pitch that had been set up in the studio. Much to the amazement of the audience George chipped the ball onto the bar, against the post or wherever Frost asked him to put it. Throughout his career television was fascinated by George Best. He is one of the few people to be used twice on 'This Is Your Life' and when he turned to punditry on Sky Sport he took to it like a duck to water.

Above: When this picture was taken at the beginning of July 1971 George had just returned to Old Trafford for pre-season training. Most of his close season had been spent in Majorca which he had discovered in the mid-60s and often referred to as "my paradise". At 25 he should have been just approaching his peak. But sadly his best years were behind him. The end of the Busby era, an ageing team, the realisation that neither Wilf McGuinness nor Frank O'Farrell had the flair for the job heightened the onset of disillusionment. When Tommy Docherty and his ego arrived, the end of the time when Man United was George's world was nigh.

Left: In April 1971 when this picture was taken George's celebrity was at its zenith. He is seen here warming up before a league game with Ipswich Town managed then by Bobby Robson. It was in the days before Robson's knighthood and when he had black hair. George also sported a black mane at this time. It seemed that it used to get longer the more he was being pursued by the tabloid press. It was almost as if he was trying to hide behind it. He was still featuring on the sports pages before and after games but he was on the front page a great deal more often. The year had started badly in that regard. George had missed the train bringing the Manchester United party to London for a game with Chelsea. He travelled down later but when he saw the posse of press at Euston Station he did a bunk. He ended up spending the weekend at the London flat of a girlfriend, the actress Sinead Cusack. The episode filled the front section of the popular press for most of the following week. The press were outside the flat in numbers. There were cameras everywhere. Inside George, and a somewhat bewildered Sinead, snuggled up on the sofa and watched it on television like the rest of us. But it merely indicated just how crazy George's life was becoming. Having any privacy was by then virtually impossible. It was around that time George started to get the urge to run away from it all and even to turn his back on football.

The Legend – in Pictures   77

Above: When George was sent off against Chelsea in August 1971 he was absolutely incensed. His crime had not been kicking out after some rough treatment by the Chelsea defence marshalled by Ron 'Chopper' Harris. Instead referee Norman Burtenshaw dismissed George for arguing with one of his team mates! It was another first for the Belfast Boy. Republic of Ireland full back Tony Dunne and Bobby Charlton are the United players shepherding George off the pitch.

Right: The 1970/71 season did not start well for George. He was sent off against Chelsea in just the second game. United immediately asked for a personal hearing and George is pictured arriving for it in this shot. But things improved and he again finished the season as the top scorer at Manchester United with 21 goals. As well as his red card he was also given the big red book for the first time that year when Eamon Andrews uttered the immortal words – "George Best, This Is Your Life!"

Above: This picture was taken of George in May 1972. It came at the end of another disappointing season at Manchester United. The dynasty that Busby built was crumbling. By his own admission George increasingly was seeking solace in alcohol. Yet amazingly he still managed an incredible 28 goals in 53 matches. Also in this month he appeared in a Rest of Europe side for Uwe Seeler's testimonial. It is an accepted fact that no other modern footballer appeared in more testimonials than George Best.

Left: It's September 1971 and once more George Best is captured on the ball. The opponents that day were West Ham United, pride of the East End, whose games with United invariably produced goals. So it was on this occasion with United winning 4-2. A satisfactory afternoon's work especially for George. He grabbed a hat trick. His happiness was interrupted the following month when a death threat surfaced ahead of a Northern Ireland game against the USSR in Belfast. Manchester United refused to let him play. A somewhat different attitude than the one the club took a month later when another was made ahead of a game at Newcastle. They left that decision to George himself. Happily the crank calls stopped and George got back to doing what he enjoyed most, scoring goals and winning football matches. He grabbed his second hat trick of the season in December against Southampton at the Dell in a 4-2 victory. Overall he ended up with 28 goals in 53 games in 1971/72. Not bad for a winger!

Above: This picture taken in April 1972 shows the Belfast Boy surrounded by four 'gangsters' who were involved in a fashion show in Manchester. One of the models is Carolyn Moore who was a former Miss England. She was one of many beauty queens who George stepped out with over the years. He was once asked why he kept going missing. "I love going missing" he grinned back. " Miss England, Miss Ireland, Miss World…" His most notorious liaison with a Miss World was with Marjorie Wallace. She later dallied with his friend Tom Jones but lacked George's capacity for discretion. This surfaced when she told a newspaper that on a scale of one to ten she rated George a three. He was immediately contacted for a response. George just laughed. "Well that's probably two more than I'd give her," he chortled.

Right: This picture appeared just ahead of the 1972/73 season. George is looking lithe, slim, fit and happy. But sadly the promise of the summer disintegrated into a winter of discontent. The reality was that United were a pale shadow of Busby's great side. Defeats at home by Tottenham (1-4) and away to arch rivals Manchester City at Maine Road (3-0) finally showed George he was fighting a losing battle. Internal rows at the club led to George being suspended and then Frank O'Farrell being sacked with Tommy Docherty taking over. It was at this stage that the possibility of George playing in America was first floated. Pele and George in the same attack! It could only happen in America. But as so often happened in the post-United years things never turned out quite as planned for George Best.

Above: George Best was never one to bear grudges. But one man he found it very hard to forgive was Tommy Docherty. On taking over at United the abrasive Docherty immediately set about getting George back on board, using his assistant Pat Crerand as his chief bargaining chip. He promised George he would be laid back about his training while he got himself fit. But ultimately he went back on his word and even accused him of turning up for a game drunk. George denied this strenuously. But he later suggested that Doc was feeling the pressure himself and needed something to take the spotlight away from him. All of that is now academic. But the end result was that it was Docherty who finally pushed George away from Manchester United. It was a sad end. Ironically for both George and Tommy leaving Old Trafford saw them say goodbye to big time football.

Left: This shot shows George in action against Everton in October 1972. Both sides were in decline as forces in the First Division at the time. United had not won the championship since 1967. Everton had done slightly better having won the title two seasons previously with a side built around the midfield axis of Howard Kendal, Colin Harvey and George's mate Alan Ball. There was to be a fourteen year gap before Everton were crowned champions again when Kendal came back as manager. For United the wait was somewhat longer with the championship not returning to Old Trafford until 1993. Mind you it has been won seven times since! But George saw those barren years coming. He always felt aggrieved that the club did not buy big enough in the transfer market to maintain the impetus set up by the Best, Law and Charlton triumvirate.

The Legend – in Pictures   85

Above: In October 1973 Manchester United granted Denis Law a testimonial game. George is pictured here with his old friend ahead of the game with Ajax at Old Trafford. The pair remained close right until George's death in 2005. Indeed the Scot was at George's bedside when he slipped away at the Cromwell Hospital in London. As an attacking pair in their United heyday Law and Best had no peers. When Bobby Charlton was added to the mix the trio became known as Manchester United's blessed trinity.

Above: The place: the Rose Bowl stadium in Pasadena, California. The date: 9 April 1978. The two principals in the photograph need absolutely no introduction. George was delighted to be asked to present Pele with a plaque commemorating the Brazilian as the best soccer player in the world. The date had been designated as Pele Appreciation Day. Afterwards a game took place between George's team the Los Angeles Aztecs and Pele's club the New York Cosmos. It was typical of the sort of razzmatazz that accompanied soccer, as the Yanks insist on calling it, in the States back then. George was able to adapt to it wonderfully well. But then he had been surrounded by hype for so long he could cope better then most. What sold him on it most that the vastness of the United States afforded him a degree of anonymity he would never again enjoy in the UK, Ireland and most of Europe. Not all British players who went to the States as trailblazers could adjust as well as George. His old buddy Peter Osgood called it a day at Philadelphia Fury when the opposing team came on to the pitch one day on horseback, wearing Stetsons, firing cap guns and generally making whoopee. Osgood apparently turned to Alan Ball and said, "That's it for me. I'm going home." And I cleaned that up!

Above: This picture of George and the author was taken in the bowels of Windsor Park at half time during the 1987 Bass Irish Cup final. In the background totally oblivious to the fact that he is in the photograph is my friend Owen Trainor. George and I sat together that day and throughout the first half he was constantly pestered by people who wanted autographs. He refused nobody. At half time we went downstairs. "You boys look like you could use a drink!" boomed a waiter. "Two teas please," said George. A cuppa never tasted better.

Left: A happy family shot of the Bests from California arriving into Heathrow in 1981. George is holding baby Calum who has marginally more hair than he tends to favour these days! Angela was George's first wife. They had met in London initially and then met again in California when George was playing for the Los Angeles Aztecs. By this stage she was personal trainer to Cher and was living in her house in Hollywood. After a stormy courtship the pair married in Las Vegas in 1978. The marriage floundered eventually on the rock of George's drinking problems. One of the most heartening things in the last years of George's life was that he managed to build up a good relationship with Calum. Indeed both he and his mother Angie were fully integrated into the Best family circle when George died. The way that Calum conducted himself at that difficult time must have made all of them very proud of him.

Above: One of George's most enduring friendships with any media figure was with Michael Parkinson. But then they went back a long way. When George broke through at United Michael was working for Granada Television in Manchester and the pair always kept in touch. This photograph was taken to launch a special night that the BBC organized to celebrate George's 50th birthday in 1996. There were special programmes, re-runs of his greatest goals and games plus an in-depth interview with the Belfast Boy at 50. The very first official book about George was written by Parkinson and in it he recalled George watching the 1974 World Cup final in his home. Holland was awarded a penalty and as Neeskens stepped up to take it the commentator apparently said, "Well who on earth would change places with him now?" George, absorbed in the moment, apparently muttered, "I would. I bloody would."

Right: Here is Manchester United's holy trinity of Best, Charlton and Law pictured at Old Trafford in the year 2000. They were receiving lifetime achievement awards. Thirty-five years after they all played together in the Reds team that won the First Division title in 1965 they were still revered at the Theatre of Dreams. In that side, George was very much the new kid on the block. Bobby was the established England international, with a penchant for long-range goals and on the brink of winning the World Cup with England the following year. Denis Law was the archetypal Scots predator. Lethal around the box, he was feared by defenders for his lightning reflexes and his seeming ability to hang in the air. Matt Busby's assistant Jimmy Murphy, who took over for a spell immediately after Munich, once said of Denis, "You could put him on a deckchair in the penalty area and he would still score goals." He and George were lifelong friends. But their dressing room humour never left them. The day George married Alex, Denis sidled up to him at the reception and said he would bet him £100 it would not last six months. At the end of that time George phoned up 'the Lawman' as he called him and asked about his money. After a long pause Denis said, "Double or quits?"

George Best – After Man Utd

Above: This is George with his second wife Alex in 2003. They are outside the House of Commons in Westminster where they helped launch a new all-party group of MPs who hoped to raise awareness of deaths by liver disease. George's problems in this regard have been well documented and after his death his family continued to raise money for the trust begun in his name. It aims to raise awareness and provide research funds into alcohol and liver related illness. The music which moved so many people who watched George's funeral at Stormont was made commercially available at Christmas 2005 with the full approval of the Best family. All proceeds from the sales of it went directly to the George Best Trust. The artists on the record, Brian Kennedy and Peter Corry, also donated all royalties to the fund.

Left: In December 2001 George became Dr. George Best when he was honoured by Queens University in Belfast. He is pictured here in the procession outside the Whitla Hall at Queens looking as proud as punch. And why not! The reality is that had football not got in the way George would probably have ended up at University anyhow. He was on the first rung of the ladder when he passed his 11 plus exam and went to Grosvenor High School not far from his home in Cregagh. However life at a rugby only school was not for this particular Belfast Boy. He missed his daily fix of football too much. So he moved on to Lisnasharragh where he was able to play football again. In some ways his recognition by Queens University merely took things full circle. It re-admitted George to a club he had been forced to leave many years previously due to his love of football.

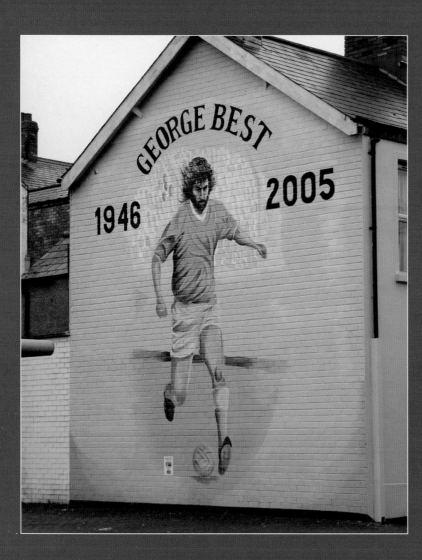

Above: George began young when it came to winning awards. He was a Northern Ireland international and had won a championship medal before he was out of his teens. He was the youngest recipient of the coveted Football Writers Association's Player of the Year award. But despite all of these there was one award which touched him very deeply. That happened back on 3 April 2002. On that day he was awarded the Freedom of the Borough of Castlereagh. A plaque, pictured here, was placed on the wall of 15 Burren Way in Cregagh, a permanent reminder that it had been the family home of soccer legend George Best.

Above: This mural appeared on a gable end in East Belfast in 2005. It shows that people in the ordinary working class districts of his native city loved George above all other footballers. It stands in the shadows of the once vibrant Belfast shipyard which sadly has gone the way of its most famous vessel the *Titanic*. But the interesting thing about George being the subject matter of a street mural is that football is not the usual subject matter of these street artists. Normally gable ends are festooned with paramilitary propaganda or scenes from the past which one group or another feels justifies their existence. But George was a person with complete cross-community appeal. In his pomp the crowds flocked from every area of Belfast and beyond, united in the desire to see his genius first hand. George Best put a smile on people's faces. He espoused the positive side of Belfast. He proved that there was a bright side of the road.

Right: This classic shot of George was taken when United reported back for pre-season training on 1 July 1968. Some five weeks previously the Manchester Reds had become champions of Europe when they lifted the European Cup at Wembley. We see George here in pristine shape. Hair neatly clipped, looking every inch the healthy young man that he was and European Footballer of the Year to boot! The first football superstar.

GEORGE BEST

22nd May 1946 – 25 November 2005

Acknowledgements

The publisher wishes to thank the following for permission to reproduce work in copyright.

© Getty Images (pp 9, 23, 24-25, 29, 87)

© EMPICS (pp 10, 13, 14, 17, 18, 22, 26, 27, 28, 30-31, 32, 33, 34, 35, 36-37, 38, 39, 40, 41, 42-43, 44, 45, 46, 47, 48, 49, 50, 51, 52, 53, 54, 55, 56, 57, 58-59, 60, 61, 62, 63, 64, 65, 66-67, 68, 69, 70, 71, 72-73, 74, 75, 76, 77, 78, 79, 80, 81, 82, 83, 84, 85, 86, 88, 90, 91, 92, 93, 95)

© John Murphy (p 94)

© Ivan Martin (p 89)